TONY CONNOR

LODGERS

POEMS

LONDON
OXFORD UNIVERSITY PRESS
NEW YORK   TORONTO
1965

Oxford University Press, Amen House, London E.C.4

GLASGOW NEW YORK TORONTO MELBOURNE WELLINGTON
BOMBAY CALCUTTA MADRAS KARACHI LAHORE DACCA
CAPE TOWN SALISBURY NAIROBI IBADAN ACCRA
KUALA LUMPUR HONG KONG

© *Oxford University Press 1965*

PRINTED IN GREAT BRITAIN BY
THE BOWERING PRESS, PLYMOUTH

ACKNOWLEDGEMENTS

ACKNOWLEDGEMENTS are due to the Editors of the following periodicals in which some of these poems have previously appeared: *Ambit, The Dubliner, Enigma, Grapevine, The Listener, The Massachusetts Review, New Statesman, Poetry and Audience, Poetry Ireland, Poetry Northwest, Solem, The Texas Quarterly, The Transatlantic Review, Trotter,* and *The T.V. Times.*

Acknowledgements are also due to Bolton Institute of Technology, The Northern Home Service of the B.B.C., and to Granada Television Network.

TO
A. J. JENKINSON
FRIEND AND PATRON

CONTENTS

Returning to himself, let man consider what he is in comparison with all existence; let him regard himself as lost in this remote corner of nature; and from the little cell in which he finds himself lodged, — I mean the universe — let him estimate at their true value the earth, Kingdoms, cities, and himself.

PASCAL

MAYOR ISAAC WATTS

Beyond my great-grandfather's bulk
of waistcoat, beard, and arrogant head,
riddle the dumb couplings it took
to raise him up, to fix his blood.

Firm, on a blanched photograph,
face set as though against light's
attrition, he is the last rough
signpost before the track fades out.

The family seeks no farther back;
issued from God Gloucester gentry
is pride-favoured. This is a rock
worth many a longer history

of shifting fortunes. Only mine
the thought that screws the foxy dark
caught in his eyes; that won't have done
until the dubious dead awake

clamouring at his shoulders. Tramp,
diddicoy, son and son conceived
at village fête or harvest romp,
the pretty maid the bailiff loved,

until she swelled,—let them appear:
fathers who drank winter away,
families that fought tooth and claw,
graceless lumps of Cotswold clay.

Kneaded together, wrenched apart
I'll see them dance: a toppling rote
of clumsy figures, gay and hurt,
then rammed home down death's throat.

For surer than recollected pride,
known quantities, titles that limn
the civil, virtuous, and well-shod,
this rabble makes the man I am

labour at poems, seeking in words
a crude power, anonymous
as all the unnumbered heads
that haunt my great-grandfather's eyes.

A WOMAN DYING

In a room with a wardrobe far too large—
bought at a sale cheap, or handed down—
this careless woman struggled for breath.
Faded oilcloth stopped short of the skirting boards;
beneath her pyjama-top there flowered
the vivid, cancerous sores. She lay with death.

Chrysanthemums in a white bowl
held their tongues, were not telling the name
of whoever had brought them. Now and then
neighbours and friends appeared to be by her side.
Her husband came, spoke, went—so did the pain;
nightdark, daylight, nightdark, and daylight again.

Already nothingness hung like a smell
among the factual furniture. The bare
bulb in its rusty socket rocked
substance away as her younger sister slept.
'Is that burglars?' she said in the small hours,
who had never worried whether the door was locked.

Something was different; something had come in
through fifty-six years of doors left on the latch,
that fed on neglected duties: dust
gathering unswept, meals she'd forgotten to make.
Perhaps it would go if she did her best:
on tiny observances she fretted dully and fussed.

But could not make redress, nor pay
attention enough to keep her sister's face
sharp as her memory of it. Trees
beyond the window waved branches of goodbye,
and then: 'What was it the branches waved?'
Question and answer were like as two peas.

3

And neither mattered. The pain blanked out
everything but a lusting after death,
or youth, or sleep—they looked the same.
Whatever knew friendly flesh was good, was God.
She choked and spat and coughed and tore
down Heaven with moans until the doctor came.

A needle eased the world away.
She did not see the window's curdled shine
grow fronds and flowers which multiplied
all night despite that thrusting, fiery, breath.
At dawn winter went on without her,
while by the bed her sister stood and cried.

FASHIONABLE POET READING

He has forgone the razor for a year
to hide from himself his mooning eunuch smile.
His eye—a disease devouring detail—
finds poems in everything. Should he fail
to feed silence to death, he might think himself queer.

Page after page his active verbs perform
their masculine tricks, his syntax bares muscles
in a fighting stance through which the poor blood thrills
a wishful dream of health. He wills
significant scale on nothings, lest his infirm

grasp of the world appal him, and his claim
to deserved fame be openly suspect. Doubt
must still be howled down: sweating, he bellows out
his repertoire. Fat and guilt
begin to dissolve. He shouts. He is glad he came.

IN OAK TERRACE

Old and alone, she sits at nights,
nodding before the television.
The house is quiet now. She knits,
rises to put the kettle on,

watches a cowboy's killing, reads
the local Births and Deaths, and falls
asleep at 'Growing stock-piles of war-heads'.
A world that threatens worse ills

fades. She dreams of a life spent
in the one house: suffers again
poverty, sickness, abandonment,
a child's death, a brother's brain

melting to madness. Seventy years
of common trouble; the kettle sings.
At midnight she says her silly prayers,
and takes her teeth out, and collects her night-things.

AT TYDDAN ALICE

A wind that sought to change the map
blew off the sea from dawn to dark,
trying the purchase of the landscape,
piercing the farmer at his work
in fields where sodden crops lay
flattened beneath a racing sky.

And now the night beyond the house
thrashes and roars as though the day
no more than limbered to unloose
a force that will blow the world away;
unwinding lanes, uprooting trees,
tumbling the mountains with the valleys.

At twelve, against the hurling black,
I shoulder my way to shoot a bolt;
barn-timbers creak that will not crack,
the cattle, still as lumps of basalt,
slumber behind hedges, sure
their tether is straight to earth's core.

Only my city-settled wits,
contriving fictions of The End
from lack of traffic-noise and streetlights,
are threatened by this night of wind,
and might be battered to destruction
were they left out in it till dawn.

All else is safe. I curse my fears
bred among brick, and hugging close
a wall that's stood three hundred years
of foul weather, regain the house,
to lie fretting the edge of sleep,
uncertain of my human shape.

7

THE AGENTS

The flowers are agents of her will.
She has set them out there to stare in
yellowly from the window-sill
while she is sleeping. Petal and stamen

receive my night-long thoughts. Stored
in damp recesses of clustered leaves
they await tomorrow's commanding word,
when they will give her back what grieves

me and makes me glad; my secret gods
and devils. Nothing escapes her knowledge:
no word's unuttered enough, no mood's
fleeting enough, but that the splodge

of tea-stain on the cloth will tell
as she rinses it, the children's shoes—
seemingly careless where they fell—
will whisper her bent head as she ties

them on to little feet. Her agents
are everywhere. I bear to sit
kitchen-bound, under surveillance
all night, only because I judge it

lesser indignity than to dream
adultery with women whom,
for my sake, she has told to mime
transports of secrecy and welcome.

THE SMELL

The smell hangs about the bedroom,
and can't be got rid of. Open door
and window, the smell will disappear
for a half-hour, then back it comes

as strong as ever. I don't like
it; part of it's me, mixed with powders,
perfumes, lotions, and hair-lacquers
from that loaded dressing-table of hers.

My smell used to be mine: a treat
to savour in a single bed,
a secret with God. Now my sweat,
sex, and gases, have been compounded

into a woman's property. Now
my smell is something she wears when
she strips herself for love. I
fear it will not be mine again.

THE POET'S ABLUTIONS .

The habit grew in youth;
   I hated them then
even more than the mouth
   I feared to open
and kept away from girls and held
my hand across to judge if my breath smelled.

I treated them with care,
   like a disease,
wishing they were not there.
   Nevertheless
guarding against further mishap
by use of antiseptics and a jockstrap.

To no avail. Pain
   I suffered for years.
Secretly in my groin
   I felt the cancers
lumping among the undergrowth
from which I turned frightened eyes in the bath.

Old sillinesses. Old
   sexual guilt
women and time dispelled
   up to the hilt,
for you my dear to crown with delight
those poor, sick, hated three I kept from sight.

Only the habit's stuck;
   laugh at me, Love,
when you are lying back,
   and I above
must loose myself with curses and begin
my soapy ritual at the wash-basin.

A LIMITING HONESTY

On the floor by the bookcase,
potted in some fibre whose name I do not know,
chubbily, amidst leaves of luminous green,
a purple bloom illustrates the verb to grow.

Yes, as from a grammar;
I do not care for it, and cannot pretend
it is more than a useful prop to my purpose:
an ease-in to a painful subject, a means to an end.

The brown earthenware jug
with the roomy, booming inside, which I lift from the shelf
to slow the poem, to take a breather,
reflects a changed world, a view of myself

I hasten to lose. The clock
ticks towards birth; near it Uccello's 'Chase'
in faded photogravure insists
the permanence of Art, and brings me the face

I had when I prised those pages
free of their staples fifteen years ago—
silly with hope. Much of sadness
cautions me from my purpose; offers the verb to grow.

Yes, as from a grammar.
A limiting honesty with which to greet a wife
back, splay-footed, from a visit,
trundling a belly fit to burst (it seems) with new life.

THE POET'S REFLECTION

I look at it in the mirror, this body
I've changed within, and seen change
for thirty-three years. I am pleased to see it naked—
as I haven't been since a child—daring to study
close detail: the sudden range
of muscle when I hold my arm rigid,
the crooked neck I was born with, the crop of pimples
that finds my shoulders a good place to grow,
and the numerous scars of accidents on the legs.
It's lost the flush of youth; psychologists, simples,
exercise, won't bring back the opening
bowler I was, or allow me to play the tricks
with it I played at twenty; still, at last
I'm learning to like it, as it runs
with imperceptibly gathering speed down the long
slope to the grave. Even the face I liked least
of all I knew has developed lines
and wrinkles—a kind of wan charm in its strong
ugliness—that I find attractive.
                               Flesh
that I've humped about for so many years,
it seems my spirit's come to terms with you!
I can flaunt you before women, give you a wash
of friendly concern, and I've lost my fears
of your filthy habits. We might do some good now.

AN EVENING AT HOME

Sensing a poem about to happen,
two letters demanded to be written.

One to a man about a dog
began clearly and ended vaguely;

the other, to a girl for old times' sake,
overstepped the bounds of propriety. My teeth began to ache.

From a single suspect raw-edged tooth
the pain spread all over my mouth

before I could stop it. Coupled with
rising flatulence, it nearly overcame faith

in my sacred calling. But back I fought
with a concentration of poetic thought

upon my desk. I almost went over
from the chair in which I'd sat to recover—

and would have done had not the lodger knocked
to say that his sink waste-pipe was blocked.

Using the plunger, I began to feel jaded
and disillusioned; something more was needed

than mere poems to right the world.
My hands were numb; I remembered the millions killed

in God's name; I remembered bombs, gas-chambers, famine,
    poverty,
and my greying hair. I could not write poetry.

My nose tingled as though it was going to bleed;
I shut my notebook quietly and went to bed.

INTERIOR WITH FIGURES

She sits reading. Caesar conquers Gaul,
half of his mind on Roman politics.
The rain drums on the outer wall;
I shift a hand, a nerve in my eyelid ticks.

As heavily still as the furniture she seems.
Pompey is Consul, Caesar has few friends.
Her feet are ugly fruit on graceful stems;
she is fresh from the bath; a cup of coffee stands

next to her on the carpet; a small stool
is under her feet. Civil war looms.
Is she carrying in her belly a girl?
Quiet, quiet, are all the closed books, and the room

is warm despite the wind and rain of night.
She is eight months gone. Caesar is marching back.
I scratch my nose. There will be a fight
when Caesar and Pompey meet. She grips the book.

A DEATH IN THE FAMILY

My father died
the spring I was twenty-five. It had been
a dragging winter. The night was cold
when a distant cousin of his we'd never seen
knocked at the door to tell us. We smiled
uncertainly at one another.
Nobody cried,

none of us grieved—
why should we? He'd been absent for too long;
even my mother couldn't find a tear
to mourn him with. She'd grown strong,
hardened against him in the twenty years
since the day he'd gone, saying he'd be back—
and she'd believed

he would be back.
My sister and I couldn't remember
much about him, and what we could
might have been false. I thought I'd clambered
towards his smile on a rumpled bed,
she felt in her hand a shilling he'd given her, but the tales
made us lose track—

tales we'd been told.
We didn't know what was ours or hearsay
so many people he'd called his friends
had stayed around us, whose every memory or stray
comment fed our starved minds.
But we never thought of his coming back,
or growing old.

'Ironic', I said
to my mother that cold spring night,
the visitor gone, ourselves at table,

'That a man can pass from all knowledge and sight
of family for twenty years. Can dissemble
completely, and yet be found-out
as soon as dead.'

This is the way
we'd talked of him always, as though he were
a case in the papers; not, I think,
to put him in perspective, but to ensure
that neither self-pity nor the rank
tendrils of guilt choked the life of the household.
Day by day

he receded farther
into the region of myth—to which,
no doubt, he'd banished us. Images
do not hurt as much as people; such
details as we gathered were appendices
to empty pages. Our only
parent was a mother.

But we were wrong,
my sister and I; my mother as well—
calling him 'John Connor', with no
suggestion she'd ever slept with him at all.
It took his death to rescue him from limbo;
to give again to an abstract evil
a human tongue.

MY FATHER'S WALKING-STICK

Swindler, con-man, and embezzler,
are a few of the roles my father played.
Declared a bankrupt in '32,
he opened a radio shop in my mother's name,
forging her signature to save time and trouble.
She was the only daughter among
a pack of lads—the last at home,
when he met her. She and a widowed mother
in a well-kept house. No wonder his lodger's eye
brightened towards the ageing girl.
Soon my grandma was baking him meat pies,
calling him 'Son'.
                It must have seemed
a good arrangement to all concerned: he,
with the urge to procreate that visits
philandering men after years of contraceptives—
but no home-making instinct, found
a home already made; my mother,
fiercely dutiful, thought she could add
a husband to what existed; my grandma
imagined daughter and self provided for.
Perhaps there was love, too. I can't
answer for that, although my mother,
even at sixty-nine's a sucker for silver-tongued men.

Snapshots show him in a cap
with a big neb, his arm round her
on a boat to the Isle of Man; both
are smiling, three months before my birth.
Later, there's one of her in a laughing pose
next to the backyard dustbin. Taken
by him, it looks affectionate—as though
he'd said, as he clicked the shutter: 'Let's
have it backwards-road-about tonight.'

17

But my mother's fervent, legal, honesty
must have shocked him. Out of bed
he couldn't persuade her to accept
his improvisations. When angry creditors
and detectives called, she jibbed at saying:
'I'm sorry, he's gone to London on business.'
According to their different lights
they let each other down badly. I was five
when he disappeared with a Royal Warrant
out for his arrest. None of us saw
him again, but twenty years on,
incredibly breaking silence, came news
of his distant death.

      Among his belongings
(the woman he'd lived with had them in a cardboard
grocery box, ready for me to claim or reject)
I found a stout walking-stick.
Thinking it apt that, having been
without support from him for so long,
my mother should have something of him
to lean on at last, I carried it home
three hundred miles under my arm.
Her comment was flat, but had an edge
I couldn't name: 'Put it in the hall-stand.'
There it has stood, unused, to this day.

MY MOTHER'S HUSBAND

My mother worries more
as she grows old, about that period
when he was at home. Not that she ever
admits to doubt of her ramrod-
straight honesty's perfect right
to feel outraged at his behaviour,
not that she says there was some wrong
on her side too—no matter how little.
The way her mind turns back
is like a child retracing steps on a dark night,
vainly scrabbling ground for the bright
coin it had gone to purchase sweets with—
unable, even, to find the hole
through which it must have slipped.

Sometimes she makes a joke
of how her conscience settled
all the bills he let go hang
when he disappeared, or of her luck
in picking such a fool
of a man from all the ones she kept
dangling from her little finger.
More often, though, she sees his criminal streak
as author of her tragedy,
unfailingly lumping with it, even now
not daring to consider longer—
his cruel trick
of being different; deliberately
taking the other side, the opposite view
from 'everyone else'. I think of my
serious clashes with her rigid mind;
her closings, with a blind:
'You're getting like your father.'

At seventy, there are certain new
infinitesimal hints of tone-
changes in the iron mockery
with which she tells of how he'd go
miles to hear a thing called 'Lohengrin',
and how she's seen him, thick with lather-
foaming from ear to ear—
posturing at the mirror like a loon,
reciting soliloquies from Shakespeare.

A DEATH BY THE SEASIDE

I

Too clearly for my comfort, I am able
to picture a likely ending for myself;
not slain by Gods, or torn apart by rabble,
or making a last insanely proud and wilful
stand against storm or sea, but rather, a quiet
lodger—the only guest—in a boarding house
where stairs are being moved, walls knocked out,
and the downstairs parlour changed to a cocktail lounge
ready for next season. A man of sixty,
or thereabouts, who writes no letters. At night,
a man who sits alone, staring fixedly
at each successive programme on the bright
screen amidst the contractor's half-completed
contemporary fittings. Type of Timon—
but not disgusted enough to be great—
I see myself, a soured old man—a 'rum 'un'
to landlady and cleaners; one whose ways,
and presence by the shore in dead of winter
are cause for speculation 'though he pays
on the dot each Friday'. One who has no banter,
and little luggage, who walks the gusty prom
sick of the past, impatient for death to come.

II

I'm thinking of my father, and the stroke
that finished him off a long long way from home.
He was a man who gorged till he was sick:
wife, children, friends, desire, Rome—

he rid himself of the lot. Moderate men
take nourishment from a diet such as this;
he was immoderate, always. He moved on,
revolted by his vomit. The curdled mess

21

looked nothing like the tasty meal he'd eaten:
it ruined his appetite. The very sight
of others' relish turned his soul. The glutton
became ascetic; he ate hardly a bite

for twenty years, and died nowty and cold,
uncared for and uncaring. In his room
a youthful policeman riffled through the old
thrillers and cowboy stories after him.

III

My teeth are good, my vision's twenty twenty,
my flesh attracts the women that I want;
at thirty-four, I am a horn of plenty,
a prodigal with riches. From this point

in time, I could believe the past a gift:
accumulated selves, (not one that's dead,
redundant, or drags-on, crippled)—hefty
schoolboys and soldiers performing in my head

the instant's deeds; but when I cut my finger
flesh gathers slowly like a ripening pod,
straining to close the fissure, 'flu takes longer
to clear, I wake in the small hours, afraid

my sons are Cain and Abel. Worse, I see
my face—that untamed creature—taking the look
of my father's in old snaps. Age is drawing me
towards him; I might repeat his mistake,

am capable of doing. Why must I mount my wife
so often her flesh cloys? Why must I play games
with the children till they irritate and bore me, love
God so fiercely that I needs must deny his claims?

22

IV

I'll exercise for extinction on a beach
empty except for some old cripple's dog,
that's left its master dangling a slipped leash
and trying to whistle. The face of Woolworths' clock—
handless, as though time itself departed
on the tail of the crowds—will help prepare me for
the nothingness to come. I'll visit martyred
heroes, and film stars, rapists, churchmen, whores,
in Madame Tussaud's; then, when I hear my blood
rumouring death's arrival, winter's fallen
Babylon of the Pleasure Park. My mood,
confirming its valedictory lack of all
regret, will fasten on the apparatus
for easing profit from the nation's fools:
the River Caves' smeared plaster, the ramshackle phallus
of Jack and Jill, the body-stinking vault
of the Fun House. And there I'll make my will,
in front of the clockwork clown whose collapsed hulk
skulks behind shutters, leering, silent, still:
'F * * * -all for anyone', he will witness me
before I shuffle back to die alone,
shrieking for human aid.
                                        Next summer he
will shriek without one added overtone.

TO HIS WIFE

Composed of shadows and damp clothing,
   the setting you have left
for me to write my poems in
   (having yourself taken
to bed), is witness of your deft
   devotion to my downfall.
I must be all for you: loving or loathing—

and either a full-time job. You crave
   every preoccupation,
detail of thought not being your care
   provided you are there.
Surely tonight, of all nights, when passion
   has heaved bodily overboard
any suspicions we had that the other gave

less than we gave ourselves, you might
   have left me to do my writing
unencumbered by this array—
   the evidence of your washday?
Whose very shadows, jutting, butting,
   menace my desk and hand—
familiars of your sleep, daring me to write

of anything but you. This token
   of servitude then: a poem
made in your image, despite
   my wish to spend these night-
hours as though this hearth and home
   knew none but me. A state
in which not the slightest whisper of you need ever be spoken.

MOTHER AND SON

I

Arrived from savage years, against hope
at this quiet time, and finding here—
despite her male-child's unforgiven rape
of her virgin motherhood—that the longed-for future

she fought to kill with fanged comforts of home,
smiles at her from its cradle, she takes on
her rightful dignity, and final fame
as favourite of a matchless, new-born grandson.

II

Watching them close together, well may he—
father and son—ponder his part in this
domestic celebration. Was masculinity
proved by the fight, or by the issue?

Or was it by this meeting he had shrunk
to less than one who drank and stayed out late
and went with women? Standing by the sink
he worries a fresh hole in his trouser pocket.

THE ODYSSEY OF THE FINGERS

I touch your arm, I slide my fingers up
from knuckle of wrist to elbow, and on to the top.
You have set no limit on where my hand must stop,

but watch its progress with a wary eye,
as though my fingers—which are twitching by
this time, like a sodden butterfly—

might leave your nakedness and go elsewhere.
And so they might. There's much they must lay bare
besides your body, much they must discover

that lies beneath the secrecy of silence
unblinking in its bland omnipotence:
detritus of the house's earlier tenants.

Now they are off. Your shoulder falls away—
an uninhabited moonscape. They are grey
in the distance of cigarette smoke. Smoke and stay,

and listen if you will. Beyond the wall
how they scutter and pounce! They poke and crawl
into the backs of drawers, they tear out the dull,

dead eyes from faded photographs. They lurch
from cellar to attic, in a frantic search
whose object is forgotten. Touch! Touch! Touch!—

they are a blind man's! They touch pots and pans,
jewellery, cutlery, books, knitting, hair-pins,
the rack-cord, chair-backs, various bones

awaiting the stock-pot. Now they are coming back,
empty and unsuccessful. They are muck-
coated and stupid and they want to stroke

your flesh. They do not know where they have been,
on what fool's errand. The search is forgotten,
their one thought to excite your lust again.

WAKING

THE incubus of nightmare is on my chest
squeezing the rib-cage in. What beast
squats on its haunches, face to mine,
waiting for me to wake, and open
eyes like an owl's—so close are his?
I lie sweating eternities
of clouded fears away until,
hearing the milkman ring the bell,
I know the customary world awaits
beyond my darkness. The incubus fits
a sticky finger into my nose
to find out where the nostril goes.
It is my eldest son—no worse—
two years commander of this universe;
an incubus which babbles 'Daddy'
over the pouchy, ageing body
which surely should be small as his
is small, and should be racing downstairs
to the kitchen fire,a nd a huge man
who laughs and laughs and says 'Hello son'.

LODGERS

THEY came with somewhere else in view,
but scrambled to retrieve my ball,
and smiled and told me tales. I grew
within their shadows: Chew, and Nall,
Entwistle, Mounsor, Mitcham, Grey—
masterful men who could not stay.

Some boozed and came in late, and some
kept to their bedrooms every night,
some liked a joke, and some were glum,
and all of them were always right.
Unwitting fathers; how their deep
voices come back to me in sleep!

I hear them mumbling through the wall
nursery prayers and drunken smut;
I see their hairy fingers maul
sandwiches delicately cut;
I smell their smoky suits, their sweat;
salute them all, and own my debt.

They came; they fidgeted; they went.
Able to settle nowhere long,
their's were the terms of banishment
that clothe the skeleton. Their strong
fathering figures could afford
little beyond their bed and board.

And yet, enough. Each exile's mite
of manhood noble in its fall
bestowed upon me, helped me write
a name on nothing. Chew, and Nall,
Entwistle, Mounsor, Mitcham, Grey—
masterful men who could not stay.

THE POET'S DISTRICT

My mind runs on, and back, and round;
routes of my childhood fixed the shape
of thought; I cannot now escape
shadowy entries, streets that wind,
alleys that are often blind.

The games I played on winter nights—
chancing a labyrinth of dark
limbos between the gaslamps—mark
me one who races fears and doubts
with bated breath, whose short cuts

are tumbling trespasses through sad
gardens abandoned by the rich,
whose hints to pursuers, roughly scratched
arrows on brick and cryptic words
only with difficulty deciphered.

Bounded by solitude, and walls,
and brews that peter out on crofts,
concealed corners, sudden shifts
of level, backs that flirt with ginnels—
double round privies—skirt schools,

deviously beneath the close
horizons of houses, through streets
grown nightmare-still, I take thought
towards that final hiding place
where someone crouches with my face

waiting impatient to be found
and freed by a swift, relieving tig.
I am small and fearful. Very big
and quiet, and cold, and unconcerned,
the tricky district of my mind.

THE SMALL HOURS IN THE KITCHEN

LAST night in sweltering heat at one o'clock
I worked again, with no one else awake.

Behind my naked back as I crouched tense
by a yellow door unmarked as innocence,

I felt the house—its corridors and rooms—
seething invisibly with my family's dreams,

As though it were a sea I dare not look back on,
deep, dark, and featureless to an horizon

unimaginably distant, and I, near-drowned,
stretching from shallows towards unknown land.

I watched my arm extending and the latch
become a shining black-enamelled patch

under my brush; I saw, almost within
my eyeballs, then as tics on the air's skin,

the million moving motes of sand-papered dust
breath raised from the floor. I smelled the waste

clogging the sewers beneath the roads that led
from me to everywhere. I walked my own head

among the sleeping race huddled in fear
in innumerable beds; I saw the same sleeper

smoking quietly in caverns underground
waiting by panelled dials for the last command

from the same sleeper treading a different dream
of noble lives made barbarous by decision.

The heat had brought a sweat out on my brow.
Making its landing run a jet came low

over the house. At quarter past one o'clock
I saw its fairy lights, and its shape, black

against flocks of cloud. I heard the refrigerator
begin to freeze again—a sullen whirr

that ate the buzz in my skull. Upon the door
I saw a mark I had not seen before.

BEYOND HINDLEY

GLANCING outside, from strip-cartoons, and Fashion,
minutiae of threats and distrust's grinning handshake,
I thought the world, or I, had gone mad;
beneath a calm sky rushed an inaccurate landscape.

The wrong train taken: very unusual.
I get my facts right: tables, times, dates,
exact amounts I lend or borrow,
inattention to detail is not one of my faults.

And so there was only a split-second mind-swimming
loss of tether, when slag heaps, stagnant pools,
clustering gritstone houses, spanked
past in blunt denial of self-evident truths.

Of course they were different features. Similar
elements recomposed. The route I know—
(pits, and pools, and blackened houses)—
survived to the east, prey only to the slow

changes of time and weather. And the woman recently
dead, the much-loved woman who sprang to my mind
at the glimpsed graveyard, had ninety mourners,
not that grubby huddle stood by a hole in the cold wind.

THREE VARIATIONS FROM BAUDELAIRE

I

Metamorphoses of the Vampire

THE mouth I longed for, like a heavy fruit
split in its over-ripeness, gaped above me,
breasts tipped by horny nipples rasped my chest;
and 'Love', I cried, 'Oh Love', while in that cavern
deep in her flesh she sucked my life away
with merciless flexings, and the fruit swung down
oilily dripping words like scented juices:
'Die further inside me, die my happy man—
no need for conscience, I am first and last.
Salvation's in my breasts, grasp at it, bite them;
God's in my womb, thrust upwards to his light,
I'm planets, constellations, galaxies,
I'm birth, and death, and love, and day and night!'

The fruit's wet pith engulfed me. In a dream
I staggered the crazy beds of endless rivers,
thirsting to screams beneath a black sun,
and toppling, died amidst my empty veins.
I woke craving the fruit; turning to kiss her
my parched lips met a lolling sack of blood
shaped like a giant doll. I fell away
through drums of spinning blackness, till the dawn
opened my eyes to the heap of dry bones
assembling by my side: a skeleton
that squawked three times, inanely, and was gone.

33

II

Spleen

THIS rainy month is sick of life. It spills
a punishment of fogs upon the town
and the town's tenants. They flicker up and down
muffled against coughs and graveyard chills.

My mangy cat seeks out a warmer bed;
her nasty body twitches—the blood's spite
has got her too. I use a night-light
against the chattering mouths of long-dead

poets who failed—the strokers of the black.
A big bell tolls; the hearth-log's nearly out;
the clock wheezes and whirrs as though in doubt
whether there's any time, and in a muck

of rancid scent the row begins again
in the next room, between the Knave of Hearts
and the Queen of Spades, bitter in dispute—
each claiming rightful credit for my ruin.

III

The Two Statues

THAT sad house: stucco painted white,
ivy and ivy's shadow scribbled upon it . . .
I think of it often.
           A maimed Venus stood
pointing a phantom finger at a wooden
summerhouse in the garden. She was marble,
half-masked by blackberries, and she wobbled
in wind, her plinth broken . . .
                I remember talk,

earth smells, cicadas, the milky way's wide track
over our heads. You wobbled too—
the ardour of our kiss unbalanced you,
or perhaps it was a stone beneath your foot
in the damp grass. You grabbed my arm
Falling . . .
           What else?
                 Your perfume in a room
with closed shutters. When the days were bright
we ate on the little balcony, watched the boat's
creamy turn. From the islands . . . always at sunset . . .
always the same clunk as it tied-up
beyond the campanile.
           Did your lip
tremble at all those hints of future sadness:
the worm in the fruit you offered to Pomona,
the worm in the second fruit, the smashed bowl?

I see those apparitions. Not to spill
one drop of sleep, they glide erect, untrembling
from room to room. They are all you, brimming
with sleep unspilled upon a hundred midnights.
You meet yourself again and again on flights
of stairs, in rooms, in corridors. You loom
everywhere—a hundred lamps snailing their gleam
about the house. You weep. No sleep spills.
The memory freezes. The house is full of pearls.

35

THREE VARIATIONS FROM PASTERNAK

I

Not Fame

FAME doesn't dignify a man,
or make him more than human; there's
no need to file every poem
as though it were immortal—the future's

unbeknown luck. To create, you must
give without stint or hope; don't conserve
what little you've got, to feed the beast
of reputation. You need the nerve

to grasp your span without pretence
of likely favour—only then
will you find love, and gain the chance
of entering the wide-open

gates of the future. Make your books
self-reliant; sturdy and complete;
the blots, omissions, and mistakes
of life are best kept out of sight.

Be private—not concerned to leave
clues for the scholars who will dog
your fading footprints. Let them prove
you more than a landscape under fog!

And leave to them the meanings: here
a victory gained, there a defeat
suffered. To them it will matter;
to you it is beside the point.

36

For you are not seeking the truth
about yourself; to understand
is not your business. Yours is breath,
and living your life out to the end.

II

Women of Childhood

WHEN I was a child I knew a seat
beside a window. From it I could lean
my long-necked body out to a green
tunnel of leaves, where bleaching noonday heat

was drenched by shadow. Onion-domed,
a church lay to the left, beyond a wall
speckled by poplars; such a lull
I thought the scene a painted picture framed

for my idle pleasure. But into it
came—always—women: alien shapes
that laughed and chattered in gliding groups
about the neglected garden. Girls whose wit

shone in the way they walked, and those
gross of imagination: guzzling wives
with malice in their mouths. My loves
and hates grew flesh, as they swayed beneath the trees

on summer noons when cherries flashed
and winked in sunlight that would never fade.
I am the man these women made;
to their wit captive, by their tongues lashed.

III

Summer in Town

Low voices in a darkening room;
sparks from a sheaf of golden hair,
as though a storm beneath the comb
bided its time of night in there.

We talk; your arm sweeps up and down;
rivers of light pour from the teeth.
Dull thunder grunts. Over the town
a heavy evening holds its breath.

And stretched-out like exhausted dogs
the streets await the coming rain.
Ready to burst a fat cloud sags
halfway across our windowpane.

The shutter creaks; near thunder crashes
a barrage of gunfire overhead;
a solitary figure dashes
into a doorway with some bread.

Then hours of silence; nothing more,
except the lightning's nervy hand
searching the sky, until, at four,
we wake to the engulfing sound

of teeming rain. Dawn comes up grey;
the last drops patter from the eaves.
Under a still oppressive sky
a tired wind mutters in the leaves

about the square, where ancient limes
burdened with blossom catch the light,
dumb critics of disturbing times
complaining of a broken night.

TRANSATLANTIC FLIGHTS

I SELDOM notice them by day,
and when I do think 'D.C.8
bound for New York out of Ringway',
my equilibrium's not upset
by the observation. I return
to prior thoughts, with hardly a glance
above at the movement of the shine
of four jets expelling distance.

Not so at night. Half-waking to
the roar of engines in the sky,
I bury my head in the pillow
mistaking the time when I must die
for scheduled flights of passengers,
settled unconscious to the vast
eclipse of my familiar stars
travelling westward low and fast.

THE end came as I drove it down the road
that leads off this one.
                    The chassis broke with a *clang*,
pitching the rear suspension on the near side
on to the ground, where it dragged for a moment or two
until I was able to stop.
                    I drove home
somehow. It stood there in the drive looking
alright—like a poem seen in a magazine
that looks alright although you read it yesterday
and know that it's crap.
                    I had to force myself
to ring the breaker, who came and towed it away,
giving in exchange five pound notes
which I took to town and spent on books of verse.

What debts are owed to Life by Art and *vice-
versa*, I thought as I placed my books upon
the shelf, remembering how I bought the car
with dollars I earned from the sale of love poems.

ENTERING THE CITY

THE city lies ahead. The vale
is cluttering as the train speeds through.
Hacked woods fall back; the scoop and swell
of cooling towers swing into view.

Acres of clinker, slag-heaps, roads
where lorries rev and tip all night,
railway sidings, broken sheds,
brutally bare in arc-light,

summon me to a present far
from Pericles's Athens, Caesar's Rome,
to follow again the river's scar
squirming beneath detergent foam.

I close the book, and rub the glass;
a glance ambiguously dark
entertains briefly scrap-yards, rows
of houses, and a treeless park,

like passing thoughts. Across my head
sundry familiar and strange
denizens of the city tread
vistas I would, and would not, change.

Birth-place and home! The diesels' whine
flattens. Excited and defiled
once more, I heave the window down
and thrust my head out like a child.

HILL-TOP AND GUY FAWKES

Not more than his nose and one eye
was showing. He lurked, as though shy
of being caught looking—like an elderly spinster
behind her curtains when a wedding goes by.

Before we saw him seemed like an age
of fishing become shove and nudge;
one of the boys shouted, and there he was poking
slyly dead through the looped-back scum on the lodge.

The police came with iron hooks.
They shooed us off. We made tracks
behind the rusting dump of machinery
and, still as cogs among the little hillocks

of clinker, watched while they dragged him out.
The newspaper said he was seventy-eight,
'of no fixed abode': we played at being vagrants
the rest of the summer holidays, hobbling about

with sacking on our feet, and caps
held out for pennies. Then the shops
began to sell fireworks, and in our fathers' cellars
we laboured to build the burnable human shapes.

In the North of England a lodge is a small reservoir beside a mill.

LOVERS IN CLOWES PARK

THE Hall decayed, and then came down;
the corporation bought the parkland:
tree and wall, lake without a bottom
and fabled pike within it, grown

large as a man. We are late
upon the scene; the nursery garden—
rose and chrysanthemum growing over
the great family's abandoned site—

itself's abandoned. The giant fish
is quite discredited since the waterworks
dredged and restocked the weed-grown shallows
whose depth is known to the inch. That flash

of late sunlight is off the glazed
bricks of the 'Ladies', nestled in privets,
and by the soggy path a bulldozer
dozes amidst the earth it's raised

to lay new drains. The evening sky
disgorges chemicals in silence;
leaves and grasses bend, ever so little,
under each new moment's weight. My eye,

encountering yours, takes comfort from
the falling soot between, the public
neatness of squalor. Not unworthy,
as last we have come home to our true kingdom.

LANCASHIRE WINTER

THE town remembers no such plenty,
under the wind from off the moor.
The labour exchange is nearly empty;
stiletto heels on the Palais floor
move between points of patent leather.
Sheepskin coats keep out the weather.

Commerce and Further Education
won't be frozen. Dully free
in snack bars and classrooms sits the patient
centrally heated peasantry,
receiving Wimpies like the Host;
striving to get that Better Post.

Snow on the streets and Mini-Minors
thickens to drifts, and in the square
from dingy plinths, blind eyes, stone collars,
the fathers of revolution stare,
who, against pikes and burning brands,
built the future with bare hands.

F.O.S.

Day-Release, Bolton

THE present's a flickering hole in darkness,
big enough to stretch in, and yawn,
to kick a ball around on Sat'days—
not cramping-small, to rub the skull bone

as it might with a saint, till brains burst
into God's own flowers of pure fire,
nor big enough to act history out
of countenance. It is the clear

length of a croft across when the pass
comes to your boot, and the piled coats
flatten before your power. It is
as certain as pop tunes, as tits

you almost grope on the back row.
It hangs like a hood around your eyes
watching 'Commercials'. Dull and empty,
it is the dead dumps of Sundays.

And now my problem sits in the middle,
like the rain's tick on the window, the face
I turn towards you from the board.
The flickering hole becomes a fuzz

of rubbed-out things, choking like chalk
this morning room's span of now.
Able neither to shake off nor
pull down the darkness, must I deprive you?

MRS. ROBINSON AND MR. SMITH

HER husband dead, her children growing fast,
what could she do but take him when he came?
The look of him was queer, but she had lost
fastidiousness by then. Her care was formal:
Could she see his references?—the house had a good name.

The postcard she had placed a month ago
in the newsagent's case had brought her no replies.
She knew she must not let him get away,
and stated terms apologetically,
shocking herself by bringing to her eyes

that winning smile—she quickly cut it dead—
from which her husband in the early days
had taken his liberties. Standing with bald head,
cheap cases dripping on the lobby floor,
the man said he was tidy in his ways,

kept early hours, and took a little drink,
speaking as though the words were preordained
by greater powers. Whatever she might think,
they were unalterable. She sensed a will
stronger than hers—though burdened heavily, and chained.

His name was Smith; he was a Clerk of Works;
when he was young he'd lived with maiden aunts;
he had a wife and child in Halifax,
but didn't see them; they led separate lives;
he'd once worked in America, on a ranch,

a long time back. Such answers as she gleaned
were not from questions asked; he was a man
she could not question. Yet her silence learned
to put an edge on his, till he must tell
more than he meant to. With the children gone

to bed they'd sit together in the room,
she knitting in her husband's favourite chair,
he chain-smoking despairingly, and dumb.
Until, as though in wilful disobedience
of orders that were more than flesh could bear,

he'd speak of his past in toneless, guilty blurts
of disconnected detail. She would make
a pot of tea, and wonder what deceits
he practised on himself, or her, or both,
for there was nothing to explain the sick

terror that drenched his face when he had done.
She—who remembered how her husband laughed;
his open way, his jacket pockets clean
of any secrets from her when he died—
dreamed now of this other. In her soft

acres of empty bed she wrapped him round
in God's forgiveness, when, by being freed
of so much that was silence, he demeaned,
austere and mighty-willed to take her tongue,
and mount her vastly, and fulfil her need.

They never touched. He brought her now and then,
on Sunday mornings, tea and toast, in bed;
always attentive—though the door was open—
for his knock to wake her. She would rearrange
the blankets smooth and tight, so that her head

was all that showed. They took to playing Whist
on winter nights. Sitting there face to face,
she knew she would never have him. Rain hissed
in the fire, the only other sound the tiny
plop of queen on knave of ace on ace.

The possibility had passed. What might
have been from clues he never gave
evaporated in the twitching firelight.
Coherent and quiet, now he spoke
of work and works' affairs; of Joe and Dave

he'd had to sack; of girls in the canteen—
flibbertigibbets. She, incredulous
at memory's giant dwindled to a mean
guardian of clock-cards and of bosses' profits,
began to wish him gone from her husband's house.

In Spring the site was finished. At the door
they said goodbye. He fiddled with his nose,
and shook her hand. She watched him disappear
round the street's corner, then went back in the house,
and scrubbed his room and opened all the windows.

ALEX AT FORTY

I FIND him in the spare room,
curled on a mattress on the floor,
another over him. His face
is pouched, he snores amidst the reek of beer.

At ten in the morning, still flat,
with last night's revelry curdled to
a nasty mouth, he opens pig-
eyes on a crumpled suit, a new day.

Blearily to our fire (there's nothing
owing) he comes to make his peace
on stinking feet. My wife is polite
but disapproving. He coughs, he hems and haws,

abject and arrogant by turns.
Apologies twist his mouth like insults:
he laments his squandered gifts, his thirst,
family pride, guilt, and all Celts—

but borrows ten shillings. Half inclined
to hate my job—the monthly cheques
with which I pay the bills, I buy
a poet's share in the dog-rough fall of Alex,

who leaves at eleven: Opening time.
I watch from the window. In the street
his step recovers its jauntiness.
My wife serves coffee, bitter as defeat.

JOHANNES JUNIUS, 1528

from Bamberg Prison:
      '... turned me on a spit,
I thought that Heaven and Earth were at an end.
Beloved daughter ... this, my last goodnight;
tomorrow they will kill me, but believe
your father innocent, though I confessed
to witchery from fear of greater pain.
It is alike with all those now accused
who lie here with me. Six, before they died,
asked my forgiveness in God's Holy Name—
they had confessed against me.
      There are some
whom I must ask forgiveness of; the same
have I screamed-out upon the rack ...
no man is safe from pain's promiscuous tongue.

Dear child, they are all lies and made-up things—
God pity him who can bethink no wrong
to stay the torturer's hand, for be he ne'er
so good he shall not die until a witch.
My part is nearly done; there is the fire,
and then an end.
      I am too weak to fear
further these holy men who feed their God
their neighbour's broken bones and burning flesh
that they sleep sweet of nights.
      I shall be dead
when you receive this letter ... pray for me—
no prayers are left in this foul place
but those of blood and madness ... pray for me.

I cannot write you more ... my hands ... my eyes....'

ALBERT HARPER

THE first thing we did, we took the huge old mirror
from the hall, and smashed it into pieces
by the dustbin.
    That was on Monday.
        Then
we got to work and cleared the cellars out:
strips of oilcloth, rotted; a skeletal mouse;
a heap of odd-shaped lengths of wood; a picture
of hussars, or someone, sitting in rows;
and an old mangle that had to be dismantled
before it would come up the stairs. After that
we felt easier, having a known emptiness
under our feet.
      We were living in the kitchen—
which we'd finished in white flat paint and red gloss,
with a porcelain sink and built-in cupboard space,
and the latest gas stove. The bedroom was as bad
as the rest of the house, but being always asleep,
or twined together laughing, we didn't care.
My wife was busy making curtains by day,
or trying to find things that we'd lost in moving,
I laboured prising numberless nails from floorboards,
so when she said she wanted to sleep in the attic
I thought she thought I'd been neglecting her,
and this was a woman's way of striking back.
But 'No', she said with a light kiss and a smile,
she wanted me there too. She likened the attic to my head,
and said this was her chance to dream in it.

I'd been expecting yearnings after olives,
or walnuts—which my mother says made me
emerge coated in husks—or yams, but not
a whim of this kind. Still, it helps to air

the house right through, I thought, and up we went.
Attics have always frightened me. A woman
who lived across the street when I was small
hanged herself in one. I never open
a door high in a house without some fear
of what I'll see, and here it was the same
despite the pretty curtains and her air
of absolute assurance while she waited.

The bed was low; we put bricks under it,
one to each corner, for the midwife's sake.
(There was a gardenful of porous bricks
half-hidden in the weeds that summer brought)
I thought her temper might be sweetened so,
forgetting that the stairs would be enough
to justify her usual sourness. She
drew out a baby boy, as though he were
the core of a carbuncle.
                            Later, that was,
after I'd stripped the hall, repaired the broken
window-cords, and paid for new gutters.
He came on Sunday when the sky was blue,
and I was watching cricket down the road.
The difference was the room seemed luminous,
or perhaps it was my head.
                            I can't remember
clearly what happened then: success, of sorts,
at work; a rockery I nearly built;
some holidays; the way the hawthorn caught
the light on summer evenings; frozen pipes;
that pram we sold to people in the papers;
until one day I visited the cellars,
and found them full of half-forgotten things.

My son was with me; there had been a flood.

I must have put them down there, but they seemed
like variegated fungi sprouting from
the cloggy alluvium.
                    He was after girls,
and left me to the junk and dirt we'd gathered
in sixteen years.
                    I thought of how we'd cleared
the cellars out when first we came. The years
didn't return in any detail—just
some few weeks when first we settled in.
She was a strange girl then, and now the attic's
a billiard room where him and all his mates
chatter away the evenings.
                    Still, I thought,
he's started to take a pride in his appearance;
his mother must have noticed.
                    Those hussars!
I wiped my boots and went upstairs to tell her.

OLD BESWICK

Always death's companion—bearded,
stooping to earth and mumble-worded
with flower heads, dug-up roots, the hutched
rabbits he fed on crisp lettuce and grass fetched
each day fresh from his nursery garden—
he was the terror of my childhood. Forbidden
things lurked in the steam behind his patched
greenhouse glass; both his legs were wooden.

It took years of my growing-up
to cleanse from sleep the bedraggled gap
in a hedge through which, with a mouthful of curses,
he came at me once, his pee-stained baggy trousers
slapping those rigid limbs. A lad
told me all of him was turning into wood—
his own coffin, the kids whispered. Houses
were safe and so were streets; I stayed in and read,

and played amidst the comfort of alleys,
blotting his holy of black holies
out of my mind with hopscotch, tig,
Masterman Ready, errands with basket or jug,
and homework. Never daring to trespass
again in that part of the park where an ivied buttress
leant on the Hall's remaining wall—a sag
and stagger of crystalled brick bounding the monstrous

garden where he, flowers, steam,
rabbits, and death, kept bloodstopping company. Time
plays strange tricks on memory: he married
a young widow, when I was twenty and hadn't worried
or dreamed about him for years. His face,
elderly and benign, smiled from the close
print of the local paper, but my sleep was harried
anew by the old evil, roaring its curse

on all imposture, the open furnaces
of its eyes dazzling the lake, and the houses
beyond the gates, as I ran and ran
away through the years, and on on on
came the wooden legs, lurching the fiery
twilight at every step, till the mouth, hairy
and vast as God's cried, 'Perish the man
that takes my name in vain', and I woke in a fury

of sweat and sheets, sure that death
for the old man had burst from the pith
of a child's nightmare into the present,
and through the dawn-wet streets hastened
that moment towards his marriage bed.
He lived for years longer. People said,
when he died, that but for arthritic hips there wasn't
a thing wrong with him; what an end for a good

old soul—to slip and fall in the nursery
garden he'd made his life! Wary
of whatever was to disturb, I kept
away for ages. Then, on a day nipped
by autumn's first teeth, returning
from somewhere beyond the park, I smelled leaves burning,
and trod again the familiar path between lopped
columns, fallen corbels, and ironwork turning

wholly to rust in bushy grass.
Silence; and woodsmoke curling across
a waste of weeds. In seeding cabbage
the hutches were random planks. A heap of garbage
rotted amongst the broken pipes
of the caved greenhouse. I wondered what hopes
proved false, as I walked—devoid of fear or courage—
towards the young keeper's fire by the small copse.

THE POET'S AGE

It visits you at night. You have awakened
from damp, barbarous dreams to this worse thing
haunting the house in which your family sleeps.

You cannot see, or hear, or feel it, although
the black becoming lumpy with your possessions,
the small sigh from the cot, even your wife's

delicate flank against your rough flesh,
are terrible in its presence. You will not rise
to seek assurance from your poems. Lying

breathless with fear you know they were not worth it.
You will not rise to smile upon your son.
He is growing towards your death. You will not turn

to find companionship; you had young loves,
but that was long ago. You sweat in a staring
silence through which the rolling planet speeds,

you and that thing you jollify with birthdays,
dignify with position, charm, and honours,
you and this lustful, ravening, killing thing.

LODGERS